Marga

April

Picturesque
YORKSHIRE

painted by Gordon C. Home
and Warwick Goble

KIRKSTALL ABBEY, LEEDS

SALMON

Published by
J Salmon Limited
100 London Road, Sevenoaks,
Kent TN13 1BB

First edition 1995

Designed by the Salmon Studio

Paintings by Gordon Home
reproduced by kind permission
of A. & C. Black Ltd.

Printed in England by
J Salmon Limited, Tubs Hill Works
Sevenoaks, Kent

BEVERLEY MINSTER

Coloured Illustrations

All paintings are by Gordon Home unless shown

STONEGATE, YORK

The Market Place, Ripon

THE THREE MINSTER TOWNS
York, Ripon and Beverley

To stand upon the walls of York, whether in the early morning sunshine or when the shadows are falling on the red roofs and grey gables, is to live through two thousand years of history. No man should foster a delusion that he can see and know York in a week, a month, even a year. There is always something to find in her which has not been found before – some quaint bit of architecture, some newly discovered relic, some unseen corner.

Once in York one naturally turns first to the great Minster Church of St Peter, whose three towers are seen for miles over the level land which lies outside the city. Like most of our great English cathedrals it has its special delights – the tomb of Walter de Gray, the Five Sisters Window, the wonderful Chapter House, the Saxon work in the crypt. But its chief beauty lies in its majesty; other cathedral churches may be more picturesque, but none fill the senses with such an impression of power and grandeur as does this of York.

Travellers who love old buildings will find much to savour in York. In the grounds of the Yorkshire Museum are the ruins of St Mary's Abbey, one of the most important monastic houses in Yorkshire. Round about the Shambles there are houses which seem impelled by a desire to fall in upon each other, and magnificent specimen of a fine old timbered house exists in

Beverley Minster

St William's College at the east end of the Minster. The evidences of antiquity in York are everywhere.

Ripon and its little cathedral, visible for miles around, stand at a point where the fells cease and the country is a green, agricultural landscape. It is a pleasant town, with a large market square in which many of its older houses are preserved; it is said to be the second oldest town in England. Ripon should be better known than it is. Nothing could be more peaceful than an evening in and about the market place, in the precincts of the cathedral, or amongst the streets near the Skell.

Yorkshire boasts three great patron saints – St William of York, St Wilfrith of Ripon, and St John of Beverley. To St John, Yorkshiremen owe the incomparable and beautiful Minster, which is the glory of the East Riding. Many would unhesitatingly declare its west front to be the finest in this country. Beverley possesses a distinct charm of its own and it is a quaint little town set in level land on the edge of the Wolds; a town of red roofs and gables and a picturesque market place. Once surrounded, like York, with walls, it is strange now to think that it was then a port on the River Humber and sent ships to sea.

YORK FROM THE MINSTER

BOOTHAM BAR, YORK

ST. MARY'S ABBEY, YORK

THE MARKET PLACE, BEVERLEY

RIPON MINSTER FROM THE SOUTH

FOUNTAINS ABBEY, SKELLDALE

At Bolton Abbey

THE YORKSHIRE DALES

Nearly the whole of the Dale country lies in the North Riding and within its confines one finds most of the delights which have made the Yorkshire Dales famous all the world over. Of what the lover of beauty may find in this landscape it is difficult to tell within narrow limits. Swaledale, Wensleydale, Nidderdale, Wharfedale and Airedale are not merely valleys where one finds beauties of scenery; they are distinct tracts of English country, each with a character and features of its own, a history of its own, and an atmosphere which is peculiar to itself. Each of these dales too is rich in associations of an historical, or a literary, or a romantic nature; there is not one of them in which are not found the ruins of great castles, powerful religious houses, or ancient mansions, and in most of them one comes at intervals into the midst of an old-time market town whose aspect is that of the sixteenth rather than the twentieth century.

The roofs of the churches and cottages are always of the local stone, weathered to beautiful shades of grey and green. The villages of the fells are often exceedingly quaint, and by the edge of five rivers that pour downwards in terraced falls one finds hamlets with their church towers, grey and sturdy, and the little patch of green shaded by ash trees, all made diminutive by the huge and gaunt hillsides that dominate every view.

The five great dales have a geographical feature in common in the fact that the rivers, which run through them and lend much charm and character to the scenery, all finally fall into the Ouse, Yorkshire's great central stream, in country which by its own lack of feature accentuates the beauty of the Dales. No-one who sees the Aire at Leeds could believe it is the same river which one wonders at a few miles beyond Skipton or at

Bolton Castle

Malham Cove. The tameness of the Wharfe at Cawood in no wise suggests its glories at Bolton Abbey; the Nidd at Skip Bridge promises nothing of the beauties which surround Knaresborough; the Ure is a placid, homely sort of river when seen at Boroughbridge, but full of romance and poetry as it passes through Wensleydale, and receives the waters of the Skell from mystical Fountains Abbey; while the Swale, of little consequence at Myton where it joins the Ouse, is of all the Yorkshire rivers the most romantic as soon as the wonders of Easby Abbey and impressive Richmond are reached.

HARDRAW FORCE, WENSLEYDALE

A JACOBEAN HOUSE AT ASKRIGG, WENSLEYDALE

JERVAULX ABBEY, WENSLEYDALE

AYSGARTH FORCE, WENSLEYDALE

MUKER, SWALEDALE - A STORMY AFTERNOON

RICHMOND CASTLE, SWALEDALE

KNARESBOROUGH, NIDDERDALE

HUBBERHOLME CHURCH, WHARFEDALE

THE RUINS, BOLTON ABBEY, WHARFEDALE

GORDALE SCAR

THE MARKET PLACE, SETTLE

HAWORTH – HOME OF THE BRONTËS

THE COURTYARD OF SKIPTON CASTLE

THE OUTERMOST POINT OF FLAMBOROUGH HEAD

Runswick Bay

THE YORKSHIRE COAST

There are a hundred ways of seeing the Yorkshire coast. Some people go to Scarborough, or to Whitby, or to Bridlington, and content themselves by staying where they are put down. Others make a centre of one or other of these places and take excursions into the surrounding country. Here the Yorkshire coast has a great advantage over the sea border of most other counties for from any one of the principal towns and villages along its ninety miles one can quickly reach some inland scene which is more than worth seeing. From Withernsea one may explore the wonderful churches of Holderness; from Bridlington the Wolds; from Scarborough the charming scenery of Forge Valley and Hackness; from Whitby the valley of the Esk and its surrounding hills.

It is impossible, within brief compass, to tell anyone what to see on the Yorkshire coast – the delights are too numerous. But the real way to experience the area is to start out from Hull, and to journey thence as far as Patrington and subsequently to Withernsea, afterwards following the coast northwards to the mouth of the Tees.

There is an immediate reward in following this route; no-one can say that he knows Yorkshire unless he has seen the two glorious churches of Hedon and Patrington - the 'King' and 'Queen' of Holderness.

Scarborough Castle

To some people the most noteworthy place on the coastline will certainly be Flamborough Head, with its light-house perched 250 feet above the sea. To ascend the headland on a winter's day, when the winds are howling and the seabirds screeching, and all Nature seems alive with storm and wreck, is an experience not soon to be forgotten. Northward the cliff scenery is the most striking, the chalk faces rising to a height of 450 feet at Bempton before dropping away to terminate at wave-lashed Filey Brigg.

Scarborough is not merely the "Queen of Watering Places" but an ancient borough of historical associations. There is the town itself, with its quaint streets and old houses, there is the castle, and there is a fine old church where Anne Brontë is buried. From Scarborough one journeys to Robin Hood's Bay, a picturesque place wherein lovers of the smell of the sea will enjoy quietude and beautiful air to their heart's content. In Whitby one finds one of the most strikingly situated places in England, and a wealth of historical associations, most notably its Abbey, bold and striking on the clifftop. Beyond are little Runswick, with its cottages looking for all the world as if they had been designed to fall in upon one another, and Staithes, shut in from the sea by Colburn Nab and Penny Nab, where Captain Cook was apprenticed.

PATRINGTON CHURCH

FILEY BRIGG

SCARBOROUGH HARBOUR AND CASTLE

ROBIN HOOD'S BAY

THE RED ROOFS OF WHITBY

WHITBY ABBEY

EAST ROW, SANDSEND

A SUNNY AFTERNOON AT RUNSWICK

SUNRISE FROM STAITHES BECK

THE WEST FRONT, BYLAND ABBEY

On the North York Moors

THE NORTH YORKSHIRE MOORS
and the River Derwent

Between Malton, Pickering and Helmsley is the country known as Ryedale, full of villages of character, of marvellous scenery, and with the crowning glory of Rievaulx Abbey. Malton, on the Derwent, is the little capital of the district, and makes a good centre for full exploration of the moors and wolds. Of all the principal Yorkshire rivers the Derwent is probably the least known, and at the same time one of the most interesting. Yet no-one can say that he has good acquaintance with the eastern side of Yorkshire unless he has traversed the course of this river from its two sources, past the Aytons, through Forge Valley and the lovely Vale of Derwent, with Kirkham Abbey, and the site of the historic battle of Stamford Bridge, fought on September 25th 1066.

Helmsley is one of those little market towns which one can find nowhere else in the world but in England. There is a market square, there is an old castle, there are old houses and old-fashioned inns; tall trees stand sentinel and a murmuring stream runs through the

Vale of Derwent

town to lose itself in the Rye. But it cannot hold you long when Rievaulx Abbey is but two miles up the lane in one of the most remarkable and romantic situations it is possible to conceive. The Yorkshire abbeys, more than any others, are blessed in their surroundings and the mere approach to Rievaulx is of a loveliness that touches the heart. In more pastoral country stands all that is left of Byland, another of the Cistercian houses.

Pickering, a dignified grey-and-red old town set between the moors and the wolds, is another good centre; the moors are on its north divided by the five idyllic dales of Bilsdale, Bransdale, Farndale, Rosedale and Newtondale. The ruins of Pickering Castle, the home of kings when Scarborough was but a village, may be seen on a little hill above the town.

It is almost impossible to conceive of a more delightful excursion than one which may be made in the north of Yorkshire by following the line of the Hambleton and Cleveland Hills from the neighbourhood of Thirsk as far as Guisborough and south into the wild moorlands amidst which the River Esk has its source. One may safely assert that in certain seasons of the year – notably in the fulness of spring and the ripeness of autumn – there is no part of the country which is better worth seeing. It affords a combination of hill, moor, river, woodland and crag; it is rich in old ruins and quaint dwelling places; it embraces the most varying views.

THE MARKET PLACE, HELMSLEY

KIRKHAM ABBEY, VALE OF DERWENT

RIEVAULX ABBEY

ON BARNBY MOOR

GOATHLAND MOOR

THE CLEVELAND HILLS ABOVE KILDALE